Key To Gray's Ale Brewers Assistant

James Gray

In the interest of creating a more extensive selection of rare historical book reprints, we have chosen to reproduce this title even though it may possibly have occasional imperfections such as missing and blurred pages, missing text, poor pictures, markings, dark backgrounds and other reproduction issues beyond our control. Because this work is culturally important, we have made it available as a part of our commitment to protecting, preserving and promoting the world's literature. Thank you for your understanding.

Sold only with the Instrument.

KEY

TO

GRAY'S
ALE BREWER'S ASSISTANT.

BY JAMES GRAY.

MADE FOR THE INVENTOR,
BY
P. STEVENSON,
Instrument Maker to the Honourable Board of Excise for Scotland,
9 LOTHIAN STREET, EDINBURGH.

Entered in Stationers' Hall.

EDINBURGH:
PRINTED FOR THE AUTHOR,
BY A. MURRAY, MILNE SQUARE.
1848.

TO

CHARLES DICK, ESQUIRE,

SIR,

My connection with you, in the capacity of Brewer, must be my apology for dedicating to you, as I hereby do with all respect, my ALE BREWER'S ASSISTANT, which I am persuaded will be found to be of the greatest service to the Practical Ale Brewer.

I have the honour to be,

SIR,

Your obedient Servant,

JAMES GRAY.

EDINBURGH,
March 28, 1848.

PREFACE.

Up till the present time little has been done to assist the practical Ale Brewer by Treatises on the art of Brewing. There have, indeed, been numerous works on the subject, but they have been either too large or too difficult to be understood by the generality of Brewers. If the Brewer has derived little assistance from Writings, he has derived still less from Instruments; the one now offered to him being only the *second* invented for his aid. It may surprise the public, and even some scientific men, to be told that it was not till 1784 that the first Instrument in Britain, invented to assist the Brewer—the Saccharometer—was brought forward by Mr John Richardson, Brewer at Hull. And now in 1848, I, a practical Brewer in Edinburgh, beg leave to bring under the notice of the profession the *second* Instrument, under the name of Gray's Ale Brewer's Assistant.

The Saccharometer, since its introduction, has undergone several alterations which, in the opinion of many Brewers, have enhanced its value. It now indicates degrees of specific gravity. My Instrument is constructed to work along with the Improved Saccharometer, and I humbly submit that a practical Brewer, with an average knowledge of his business, if he guides himself by the Saccharometer and my "Ale Brewer's Assistant," will have no difficulty in conducting successfully his operations, whether on a small or on a large scale.

The Saccharometer indicates what a Brewer *has* extracted from a given weight of material,—"Gray's Ale Brewer's Assistant" indicates what a Brewer *should* extract from a given weight of material. It is well known to every practical man that this has been an impossibility hitherto. Such it is stated to be in the latest published work on the subject. "To know before mashing," says Mr Roberts, in his "*Scottish Ale Brewer*," of which a new edition was published only last year,—"To know before mashing the quantity of extract which can be obtained from each quarter of malt, is a matter of impossibility even to the most experienced." This is an impossibility no longer. The Instrument now offered by me to the Brewer supplies what has so long been a desideratum in his art. My "Ale Brewer's Assistant" consists of an *experimental* part, and a *practical* part. These I have more minutely described in the body of the "Key." I would only here remark that it is not necessary that the Brewer should experiment, unless he wishes nicely to ascertain the quality of his malt. He may work all his life long with only the practical part, for the Instrument is so constructed, that the Brewer, having once come to the knowledge of the average quality of his malt, and wishing to know what extract he ought to obtain from a different quality of grain that may have been put into his hand, can easily determine the question, by taking a higher or lower quality upon the scale.

I feel confident that my "Ale Brewer's Assistant" will contribute much to the mutual satisfaction of masters and servants. For instance, a master, not a practical Brewer, who may have invested a large capital in Brewery, with "Gray's Ale Brewer's Assistant" in his possession, can determine the quality of the material he purchases, the quality of what he puts into his brewer's hand, and the extract that ought to be obtained. The Brewer, too, can determine the quality of the material he receives to operate upon, and the amount of extract it should produce. In this way the Instrument will preserve harmony between master and brewer, while it will afford unprecedented assistance to both.

Be it remembered, that for accurate agreement all materials in Ale Brewing should be by weight, and all liquids should be taken at specific gravity, in opposition to the too general practice of working by measure of malt, and what is commonly termed *rule of thumb*. It is high time that so clumsy a method in the art of Ale Brewing were laid aside.

"Gray's Ale Brewer's Assistant" is comprised of fifteen weights,—two rules of quality and gravity, with slides, and a graduated measure and key. In connection with which, as in Brewery, also a small mill,—beam and scales,—copper mash tun, with sparging machine,—cooler,—fermenting back and casks.

James Gray

KEY, &c.

To understand and work by "Gray's Ale Brewer's Assistant,"

Observe,

The Instrument consists of two Rules and fifteen Weights, (two are dumb, or fixed, to avoid unnecessary weight in the Instrument)—arranged in a Box in three divisions respectively marked, and indicate ounces, pounds, quarters, accompanied with a graduated measure indicating barrels; and a KEY.

The Rules indicate quarters, barrels and gravity, ranging from twenty to one hundred and thirty-five degrees, and the Key to 137·5 degrees, specific gravity. On the Rules are six qualities of malt, with their directing numbers and decimals, under each given gravity, and in a line with each quality of malt, and in the Key, 14 qualities, to be set and read upon the slide rule, and give the barrels, *raw, boiled, cold,* with their respective gravities, according to the quarters of malt under operation.

The Instrument is constructed so as to experiment upon the lowest given weight from which any good result may be expected, up to a very high degree—(as the scientific man will readily perceive on examining the first weight of the first division,—the weight being so small that it requires a dumb or fixed plate to define its quality—the weight itself being too small to bear any impression,) and from thence to be an assistant to the practical Brewer to any extent.

The first division of five weights, marked oz. or ounces, are assigned to flavour; the second five, marked L, or pounds, to hops; the third, marked Q, or quarters, to malt—the three moveable weights in this division, answering all the purposes of *five*. Each of the three divisions reading from the left hand to the right, marked

$$1, \tfrac{1}{38}, \tfrac{1}{4}, \tfrac{1}{8}, \tfrac{1}{2}, \tfrac{1}{18}, \tfrac{3}{4}, \tfrac{1}{17}, 1, \tfrac{1}{38}.$$

to be understood thus:—In the third division, marked Q, assigned to Malt, the first weight to the left, marked B. 1, $\frac{1}{36}$, Q. is the lowest degree of experiment for one quarter of malt; the second weight, marked B. $\frac{1}{4}$, $\frac{1}{9}$. Q. for one quarter, or for nine quarters; the third weight, marked B $\frac{1}{2}$, $\frac{1}{18}$. Q. for one quarter, or for eighteen quarters; the fourth or first dumb or fixed, marked B. $\frac{3}{4}$, $\frac{1}{27}$. Q. is made up by putting the weights $\frac{1}{9}$ and $\frac{1}{18}$ into the scales, and signifies one quarter, or twenty-seven quarters; the fifth or second dumb or fixed, marked B. 1, $\frac{1}{36}$, Q. is made up by two weighings of the weight $\frac{1}{18}$, and signifies one quarter, or thirty-six quarters; as you thus read or vary this division of weights, you must read or vary the other two divisions of weights, should you bring them into your experiment in the weighing of hops or flavour,—also the graduated measure, which is likewise marked

1, $\frac{1}{36}$. $\frac{1}{4}$, $\frac{1}{9}$. $\frac{1}{2}$, $\frac{1}{18}$. $\frac{3}{4}$, $\frac{1}{27}$. 1, $\frac{1}{36}$.

I will now show how to work the Instrument. *First*, experimentally—and, *Second*, practically.

FIRST, How to work the Instrument experimentally.

Various are the opinions, and contradictory the statements that have been given, respecting Extract from Malt, varying, I presume, according to the method on which the experiment was conducted, many of them giving little information to the practical Brewer; little confidence can be placed in, or help derived from, an experiment almost as limited as a counted number of barleycorns or pickles of malt, infused, it may be, as in a teapot. The large capital invested in brewery, and the nature of the art of brewing, surely justify research upon some other principle that may lead to a more practical assistance.

As I have termed the Instrument " Gray's Ale Brewer's Assistant," I must now be understood to treat with Operative Brewers, and I deem it the clearest method to give them a statement of actual experiment. He will bear in mind that all dry material is by weight, and all liquids by measure, by the barrel. The quarter of malt, 320 lbs. weight; the barrel, 36 gallons.

January 1848.

Experimented upon one quarter malt by the third mode of experiment, that is, by the third weight, marked B. $\frac{1}{2}$, $\frac{1}{18}$. Q. which signifies, B, brewer; $\frac{1}{2}$, one half of the range of experimental weights; $\frac{1}{18}$, one quarter, or eighteen quarters; Q, quarter; all the five modes having the same signification according to their respective marks and numbers. The weight of malt was then taken by the third weight, which signifies one quarter or eighteen quarters, and the extract or wort measured by the graduated measure, taking $\frac{1}{2}$, $\frac{1}{18}$, as formerly explained, for one barrel or eighteen barrels, as under:—

Heat of mash tun, taken from 150° to 154°; heat of sparge, from 180° to 190°; runs from mash tun crane, taken about mid run, 1st, 73 deg. specific gravity; 2d, 17 deg.; 3d, 7 deg.; 4th, 3 deg., as under:—

First, Taken as one quarter.

1st,	per measure	3 brls.	at	55 deg.	is 165 deg.	gravity.
2d,	„	3	„	16	„ 48	„
3d,	„	3	„	7	„ 21	„
4th,	„	3	„	3	„ 9	„

One qr.   Measure 12   243 per quarter.

Thus showing from the quarter of malt, 12 barrels at 20·25 deg., or 243 deg. per quarter. I now mixed all the four extracts together in one vessel, and found them to be, as near as the Saccharometer will indicate, 20·25 deg.

Beyond this I deem it unnecessary to experiment for practical purposes. I, however, for farther satisfaction, and to follow out the experimental principle, extracted three barrels more, after one and a half hour's infusion, which indicated by the Saccharometer 1·5 deg., which if added to the above extract, 243 deg., will increase the extract per quarter to 247·5 deg., only 2·5 short of the second quality, which entitles the malt to be ranked in the second quality, being more than one half of the range betwixt the 3d and the 2d quality, which I lay down as a rule for all the qualities of malt.

Second, Taken as eighteen quarters.

1st,	per measure,	54 brls.	at	55 deg.	is 2970 deg.	gravity.
2d,	„	54	„	16	„ 864	„
3d,	„	54	„	7	„ 378	„
4th,	„	54	„	3	„ 162	„

Eighteen qrs.   216 „   4374 „

Thus showing from the eighteen quarters, 216 barrels at 20·25 deg. or 4374 deg., which gives 243 deg. as the produce of each quarter of malt mashed. Thus the experiment, tested by the Saccharometer, indicates the malt to be of the **third** quality for practical purposes, as shown upon the *rules* for assistance in practical operations. Should the experiment be carried further, by boiling the raw wort, you are guided as to your hops or flavour by the other divisions of the weights as before directed.

SECOND, How to work the Instrument practically, or to assist the Practical Brewer.

Hitherto, as I have already observed, the Operative Ale Brewer has had little assistance, notwithstanding that he is operating upon most valuable materials, and a defect or failure would be loss to a considerable amount.

I would recal to his remembrance my observations respecting the statements that have been given by writers as to extract of malt, and I would here add, no more satisfactory or assisting have been the statements given as to *absorption*. Notwithstanding, to the success of his operations, it is most needful, in connection with *heat*, that he should possess a medium knowledge. Should he experiment upon *absorption*, he may come to a sounder conclusion than to range absorption from 27 to 54 gallons, and even upwards, per quarter or eight bushels, which I believe is so generally understood, as is six bushels the boll—(I beg here to intimate my opinion, that it would have been much better for ready practice had the quarter of malt been divided into ten bushels, instead of eight, the bushel would then have been of the weight of 32 lbs., or 320 lbs. a quarter. This is the mode I act upon in all my operations, viz., by tenths. Had monies been regulated by the same rule, malt at 6s. 4d. per bushel would at once be seen to be at 64s. per quarter, ten being a ready number to multiply or divide by)—showing a range of at least 27 gallons per quarter. This amount of *absorption*, viz., 54 gallons, I consider, with all due respect for Professor Donovan, is an error on his part, arising, as I apprehend, from the mode on which he conducted his experiments. My practice for many years warrants me in saying, that had he gone with this principle into operative brewing, he would, according to the common phrase, have *drowned the miller*. In my own experience I have found *absorption* to range between 20 and 30 imperial gallons per quarter of malt, the difference being caused by the state of dryness and manner of grinding. Anything below or above this in ale brewing I regard as exceptions.

I must now insist upon the Ale Brewer, if he would work systematically, 1st, to have his grist by weight at 320 lbs. per quarter; 2d, to have his utensils all barrelled at 36 gallons per barrel.

To Barrel Utensils.

An easy method for practical purposes for those who may not understand guaging of utensils, is to fill them brimful with water. Procure a barrel of 36 imperial gallons, draw off from the utensil, barrel by barrel, marking each barrel upon the dipping rod, either for the dry or wet dip. In showing the barrels by the dry dip, as is best for *coppers*, the rod must have a *float* fixed upon the under end. Number the rod by tens from the opposite end, with a prominent mark for every five between the tens. For other utensils by the wet dip no float of course is used. Mark the rod by tens from the under end, with a prominent mark for every five between the tens.

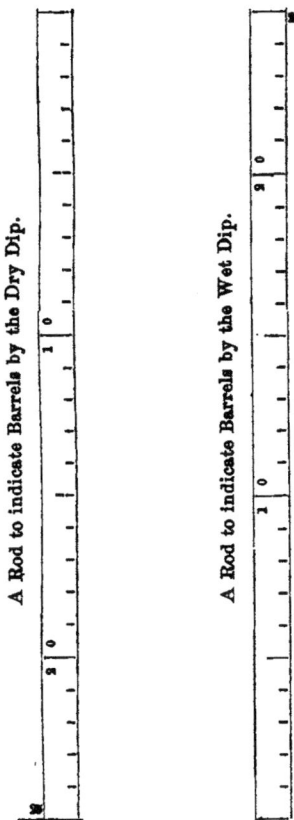

My method for readiness in practice is to have my dipping rods barrelled, as described above, which shows the barrels at once without reference to a table-book. Coppers I take by the dry dip, or by an index of barrels. Other utensils I take by the wet dip, or have an index of barrels impressed upon them. Malt I have in sacks of sufficient size to contain 160 lbs., or half a quarter, marked grist. The practical Ale Brewer, now operating upon a given number of quarters of malt, by weight, and directed to extract therefrom a given number of barrels, raw, boiled, and cold worts, with their respective gravities, having his utensils barrelled, with a knowledge of medium absorption, and applying the necessary regulated heat in his mash tun, aided by the Instrument, and working systematically, will hardly fail in bringing his operations to a satisfactory issue.

The Operative Brewer, having experimented upon his malt by "Gray's Ale Brewer's Assistant," and having found its quality to be of the third class, producing 243 deg. specific gravity, by the Saccharometer, now consults the Instrument to guide himself in the practical operation. This consists of two Rules, marked on the upper edge, No. 1, No. 2; to the left hand of which he finds marked the numbers, Q^1. D^2. L^3. Q^4. which signifies quality, degrees, pounds, quarters. The Rules indicate six qualities of malt, by the numbers, 1, 2, 3, 4, 5, 6; and the Key, fourteen qualities, with their respective degrees, pounds, quarters. In a line with which, horizontally along the Rules, and in the Key, are indicated what I term their pointing numbers and decimals, with their respective gravities, raw, boiled, cold.

The Rules indicate horizontally along the top line specific gravities from 20 to 135, and the Key to 137·5 deg. The under part of the Rules contain the slides, eight in number, two on each side of the two Rules. The upper slide is drawn from its place, and works in connection with the under slide by the stock. The under slide is not to be drawn from its place. These Rules indicate 1, or 10, or 100, or 1000, or to any extent, with their respective intervening numbers and decimals. They are marked barrels, quarters. They indicate or work thus :—

Set your given quarters by weight shown on the slide to the right hand to Φ, (or Zero) on the under stock, then look out the pointing numbers with their decimals, in a line with the quality of the malt you are to operate upon; and under the gravity that your wort is required to be in the back or tun, which gravity you will find horizontally on the first line of the Rules, or the Key, marked gravity; on the second, raw, boiled, cold, and on the third line, barrels, gravity,—barrels, gravity, —barrels, gravity. Under each of these, and in a line with the quality of your malt horizontally, you will find your pointing numbers with their decimals, which point out your barrels raw, barrels boiled, barrels cold, with their respective gravities. Then look out your corresponding pointing numbers with their decimals on the upper stock of the Rule, and under each on the slide you will find your barrels raw, barrels boiled, barrels cold.

A Practical Example.
Mashed for Small Beer.

Three quarters malt, required gravity cold, 25 deg. The malt of the third quality, experimented on as before stated. Set three quarters on the slide to the right hand to Φ, on the under stock, then under 25 the given gravity, and on a line horizontally with the third quality, you find, 1st, the pointing number with its decimal, 11·7 raw barrels, raw gravity 20·5 deg.,—2d, 10·5 boiled barrels, boiled gravity 22·8 deg.,—3d, 8·7 cold barrels, cold gravity 25 deg. Which pointing numbers with their decimals, 11·7, 10·5, 8·7, read upon the upper stock, under which, upon the slide, you find the barrels, raw, boiled, cold, which you should extract from your three quarters of malt you are to mash. Thus you work to any extent of quarters, with their decimal parts of a quarter, and to any gravity indicated on the Rules, and in the Key, which range on the Rules from 20 to 135 deg., and in the Key, from 22·5 to 137·5 deg., at fives, that is, five degrees between each gravity. The Rules are so constructed as to save unnecessary size, and to answer practical purposes readily. But should the Brewer want gravities between the fives on the Rules, he has only to consult the mean Tables in the Key, which give the gravities with their pointing numbers and decimals, a practical instance of which will hereafter be shown.

The three quarters of malt will indicate thus by the "Assistant."

Pointing Nos., 11·7, gives Raw brls. 35·0, Gravity, 20·5 deg.
    ,,   10·5, ,, Boiled ,, 31·5,   ,,   22·8 ,,
    ,,   8·7, ,, Cold   ,, 26·0,   ,,   25·0 ,,

For the satisfaction of the practical Brewer, with whom I am now treating, I here give a copy of my operations :—

Morning, 9 o'clock, the malt being emptied into the mash tun, I let on—

	Falling Heat.	Extract.	
1st Mash, 11 Brls. at 155°	142°	9 brls.	at 51 deg.
2d „ 8 „ at 168°	152°	8 „	at 17 „
3d „ 8 „ at 164°	152°	8 „	at 9 „
4th „ 8 „ at 164°	154°	10 „	at 2 „

Evening, ½ past 2, in Copper,	35 brls.	at 20·0 deg.
„ 4, Boiled,	32 „	at 22·5 „
Morning, 7, Cold,	27 „	at 24·0 „

This mash ranks in the 4th quality, 233·3 being 1·7 below the half of the range between the 3d and 4th qualities.

AN INSTANCE OF A BREWING OF ALE.

15 quarters, required gravity, 90 deg.

Following the directions already given as to the practical working of the "Assistant," your 15 quarters of malt of the 4th quality indicate thus :—

Pointing Nos. 3·0, gives Raw	brls. 45·0,	Gravity, 73·8 deg.
„ 2·7, „ Boiled	„ 40·5,	„ 81·9 „
„ 2·2, „ Cold	„ 33·0,	„ 90·0 „

Having consulted the "Assistant," I obtained the information above stated, as to my 15 quarters of malt.

My general practice in Ale Brewing is to let into the mash tun what I term brake barrels, which I have found to range from one and a half to two barrels per quarter, according to the state of my grist, and gravity of the ale I am to brew. The heat of the brake barrels I take in the mash tun, having run it from the liquor copper, somewhat higher than I require it. I generally take the heat of my brake barrels from 175° to 180° and in some cases as low as 170°. My sparge generally ranges from 180° to 190°. Having taken my heat, I instantly empty from the grist sacks a good proportion of the grist, employing two men to empty the rest during the time of mashing, which generally ranges from thirty to fifty minutes. The mash I allow to stand from one hour and a half to two hours; my sparging I generally accomplish in from three to four hours. In cases where mashes do not go well, that time will be exceeded. I generally boil from one and a half to two hours, and in what I term good brewing weather, the temperature, ranging from 40 to 50 degrees, cools in about three hours. The hops range from four to six pounds per quarter, in some cases eight pounds, and for export, to twelve and fifteen pounds, &c. Yeast from four to five pounds per quarter; when by the barrel, from one and a half to three pounds, according to gravity and circumstances. The heat of fermentation varies, ranging from below 50° to upwards of 60°.

The Thermometer and Saccharometer I hold to be indispensably connected in the art of Brewing. The heat of raw and boiled wort, when tested by the Saccharometer, I advise to be taken as high as the scale of heat, range 130°, or by some 150°, and cold wort at 60°. In taking the required dip or *barrels* in the copper of either raw or boiled wort, deduct from the full dip at the rate of *one barrel* for every *fifty* pounds weight of *hops* in the copper. As the hops may be added at twice, I advise to have the required dip and gravity of the *raw wort*, before adding the hops.

Morning 5, mashed 15 quarters malt.

Falling Heat.	Runs. Gravity.				Gravity.
154°	104	E. 1, in Copper,	Raw brls.	45·5,	75·0 deg.
154°	88	1¼ Hours,	Boiled, „	42·0,	82·0 „
152°	24	In Tun,	Cold, „	34·0,	91·0 „

Hops 60 lb. East Kent, 4 lbs. per quarter.

This brewing, including the small beer from weak worts, advances to the third quality of malt. Total extract, 240·4 deg.

Ale Brewers define their extract by the worts in the fermenting tun. This is not at variance with my method, with the exception that should they sustain loss by accident, or during the operation of Brewing, the quality of the malt is not indicated.

The extract, according to the Ale Brewer's general term, *fermentable matter*, is thus shown:—

34 brls. wort at 91 deg. is 3094 deg.
10·2 „ at 20 deg. is 204 deg.

Qrs. 15)3298(219·9 per quarter.
164·9 per boll.

This Brewing was collected in No. 3, Back or Tun E. p. 7, barrels, 34·0, gravity 91·0, set temperature 56°, yeast 60 lb., fermented 11 days, attenuated to 40 deg., highest degree of temperature 68°.

AN EXAMPLE OF PORTER.

Mash 13 quarters, 9 amber, 4 pale. Patent Malt, 170 lbs.; Hops, 169 lbs., or 13 lb. per quarter; required gravity, 75 deg.; malt taken at 4th quality.

The "Assistant" indicates thus:—

Pointing Nos., 3·7, is Raw brls. 48·3, Gravity, 61·5 deg.
,, 3·3, is Boiled ,, 43·0, ,, 68·3 ,,
,, 2·7, is Cold ,, 35·2, ,, 75·0 ,,

Morning 5.

	Falling Heat.	Extract.	
1st Mash, 25 brls, 162°	150°	16 brls.	Gravity, 79 deg.
2d ,, 15 ,, 174°	152°	15 ,,	,, 53 ,,
3d Sparge 17 ,, 165°	150°	17 ,,	,, 28 ,,

Evening 2, in Copper, 48·0 brls. Gravity, 59·0 deg.
Two Hours, Boiled, 41·0 ,, ,, 68·0 ,,
In Tun, Cold, 33·0 ,, ,, 75·0 ,,

The extract by this Brewing indicates the malt to be of the 5th quality, the extract being 217·8 deg. per quarter, but had the nature of the business allowed what is termed a return wort, for after-mashing, there might have been 20 barrels at 15 deg. extracted from the goods, or 300 deg. which would have brought up the quality of the malt to the 3d quality, being total extract, 241·5 deg. This Brewing was collected in No. 5, tun; barrels, 33·0; gravity, 75·0; set temperature, 61°: yeast, 65 lbs; fermented three days; attenuated to 27 deg.; highest degree of temperature, 75°.

An Instance of a mean Gravity, or a Gravity between the Fives indicated on the Rules, as before intimated.

Mash 10·5 quarters for Ale; required gravity of wort, in tun, 58 deg. Malt taken at 3d quality, as on the Rules, as the required gravity is 58 deg. Look up in the mean Tables in the Key, the gravity, 57·5, and in a line with the quality of your malt, as on the Rules, the 3d horizontally, and under your gravity, 57·5, you find your pointing numbers, Raw, Boiled, Cold, with their respective gravities.

The "Assistant" indicates thus:—

Pointing Nos., Raw, 5·1, gives brls. 53·6, Gravity, 47·2 deg.
,, Boiled, 4·6, ,, ,, 48·5, ,, 52·4 ,,
,, Cold, 3·8, ,, ,, 40·0, ,, 57·5 ,,

Mash, Morning 5.

Runs Falling Heat.	Gravity.			Gravity.
150°	91.	E. ¼ p. 1, in Copper, Raw brls. 53·0,	47·5 deg.
148°	64.	1¼ Hours, Boiled, ,, 48·0,	52·5 ,,
145°	0·7.	in Tun, Cold, ,, 40·0,	58·0 ,,

Hops, 42 lb. Sussex, 4 lb. per quarter.

This Brewing, there being no Beer after, the last run or extract being 7 deg., indicates the malt to be of the 3d quality, giving 239·7 deg. per quarter. This Brewing was collected in No. 7, tun; E. 6; brls., 40·0; gravity, 58·0; set temperature, 59°; yeast, 42 lbs., 4 lb. per quarter; fermented 7 days; attenuated to 37 deg.; highest degree of temperature, 62°.

The foregoing examples stand thus:—

EXPERIMENTAL.

As 1 Quarter.

1st. Mash 3 brls., at 55 degs., is 165 degs.
2d.   „   3   „   16   „   48   „
3d.   „   3   „   7   „   21   „
4th. „   3   „   3   „   9   „
          ——   ——   ——
         12   20·25   243
5th. „   3   „   1·5   „   4·5
          ——   ——
1 qr.   15   247·5

As 18 Quarters.

1st. Mash 54 brls., at 55 degs., is 2970 degs.
2d.   „   54   „   16   „   864   „
3d.   „   54   „   7   „   378   „
4th. „   54   „   3   „   162   „
          ——   ——
         216   „   20·25 „ 4374 „
5th. „   54   „   1·5   „   81   „
          ——   ——
18 qrs. 270   „   )4455 „
                                ——
                       per qr., 247·5 „

PRACTICAL.

Malt taken at 3d quality, 3 quarters for Beer, given gravity 25.

As by the "Assistant."
Pointing No. 11·7 gives Raw brls. 35·0 at 20·5 degs.
       „   10·5   „   Boiled „   31·5 „ 22·8   „
       „   8·7   „   Cold   „   26·0 „ 25·0   „

As by the Brewing.
Raw brls. 35·0 at 20·0 degs.
Boiled „ 32·0 „ 22·5   „
Cold   „ 27·0 „ 24·0   „

Malt taken at 4th quality, 15 quarters for Ale, given gravity 90.

As by the "Assistant."
Pointing No. 3·0 gives Raw brls. 45·0 at 73·8 degs.
       „   2·7   „   Boiled „   40·5 „ 81·9   „
       „   2·2   „   Cold   „   33·0 „ 90·0   „

As by the Brewing.
Raw brls. 45·5 at 75·0 degs.
Boiled „ 42·0 „ 82·0   „
Cold   „ 34·0 „ 91·0   „

No. 2.

Qu.	Dg.	Gr. Br.	Gr. Gr.	B Br.	B Gr.	C Br.	C Gr.	57·5 R B	57·5 R G	57·5 B B	57·5 B G	57·5 C B	57·5 C G	62·5 R B	62·5 R G	62·5 B B	62·5 B G	62·5 C B	62·5 C G	67·5 R B	67·5 R G	67·5 B B	67·5 B G	67·5 C B	67·5 C G	72·5 R B	72·5 R G	72·5 B B	72·5 B G	72·5 C B	72·5 C G	77·5 R B	77·5 R G	77·5 B B	77·5 B G	77·5 C B	77·5 C G	Qu.
4	300	7·0	..	6·3	..	5·2	..	6·4	..	5·8	..	4·7	..	5·9	..	5·3	..	4·3	..	5·4	..	4·9	..	4·0	..	5·0	..	4·5	..	3·7	..	4·7	..	4·4	..	3·4	..	4
3	290	6·8	..	6·1	..	5·0	..	6·2	..	5·6	..	4·5	..	5·7	..	5·1	..	4·2	..	5·2	..	4·7	..	3·9	..	4·8	..	4·4	..	3·6	..	4·5	..	4·1	..	3·3	..	3
2	280	6·5	..	5·9	..	4·8	..	6·0	..	5·4	..	4·4	..	5·5	..	4·9	..	4·0	..	5·0	..	4·5	..	3·7	..	4·7	..	4·2	..	3·5	..	4·4	..	3·9	..	3·2	..	2
1	270	6·3	..	5·7	..	4·7	..	5·8	..	5·2	..	4·2	..	5·3	..	4·8	..	3·9	..	4·8	..	4·4	..	3·6	..	4·5	..	4·1	..	3·3	..	4·2	..	3·8	..	3·1	..	1
1	260	6·1	43·1	5·5	47·8	4·5	52·5	5·6	47·2	5·0	52·4	4·1	57·5	5·1	51·3	4·6	56·9	3·8	62·5	4·7	55·4	4·2	61·5	3·5	67·5	4·4	59·5	3·9	66·0	3·2	72·5	4·1	63·6	3·6	70·6	3·0	77·5	1
2	250	5·8	..	5·3	..	4·3	..	5·3	..	4·8	..	3·9	..	4·9	..	4·4	..	3·6	..	4·5	..	4·1	..	3·3	..	4·2	..	3·8	..	3·1	..	3·9	..	3·5	..	2·9	..	2
3	240	5·6	..	5·1	..	4·1	..	5·1	..	4·6	..	3·8	..	4·7	..	4·2	..	3·5	..	4·3	..	3·9	..	3·2	..	3·9	..	3·6	..	3·0	..	3·7	..	3·4	..	2·8	..	3
4	230	5·4	..	4·9	..	4·0	..	4·7	..	4·4	..	3·6	..	4·5	..	4·0	..	3·3	..	4·1	..	3·7	..	3·1	..	3·8	..	3·4	..	2·8	..	3·6	..	3·2	..	2·6	..	4
5	220	5·2	..	4·6	..	3·8	..	4·4	..	4·2	..	3·5	..	4·2	..	3·9	..	3·2	..	3·9	..	3·6	..	2·9	..	3·7	..	3·3	..	2·7	..	3·4	..	3·0	..	2·5	..	5
6	210	4·9	..	4·4	..	3·6	..	4·2	..	4·0	..	3·3	..	4·1	..	3·7	..	3·0	..	3·8	..	3·4	..	2·8	..	3·5	..	3·1	..	2·6	..	3·2	..	2·9	..	2·4	..	6
1	200	4·7	..	4·2	..	3·5	..	4·0	..	3·8	..	3·2	..	3·9	..	3·5	..	2·9	..	3·6	..	3·2	..	2·6	..	3·3	..	3·0	..	2·4	..	3·1	..	2·8	..	2·4	..	1
2	190	4·4	..	4·0	..	3·3	..	3·8	..	3·6	..	3·0	..	3·7	..	3·3	..	2·7	..	3·4	..	3·1	..	2·5	..	3·1	..	2·8	..	2·3	..	2·9	..	2·6	..	2·2	..	2
3	180	4·2	..	3·8	..	3·1	..	3·5	..	3·5	..	2·8	..	3·5	..	3·2	..	2·6	..	3·2	..	2·9	..	2·4	..	3·0	..	2·7	..	2·2	..	2·8	..	2·5	..	2·0	..	3
4	170	4·0	..	3·6	..	3·0	..	3·3	..	3·3	..	2·7	..	3·3	..	3·0	..	2·4	..	3·0	..	2·8	..	2·3	..	2·8	..	2·6	..	2·1	..	2·6	..	2·4	..	1·9	..	4

Above the Rule: rows Qu. 4, 3, 2, 1 (Dg. 300–270)
Qualities on the Rule: rows Qu. 1, 2, 3, 4, 5, 6 (Dg. 260–210)
Below the Rule: rows Qu. 1, 2, 3, 4 (Dg. 200–170)

No. 4.

1	2	Gr.				112.5					117.5					122.5					127.5					132.5					137.5					1	
Qu.	Dg	R		B		C		R		B		C		R		B		C		R		B		C		R		B		C		R		B		C		Qu
		Br.	Gr.	Br.	Gr.	Br.	Gr.	B	G	B	G	B	G	B	G	B	G	B	G	B	G	B	G	B	G	B	G	B	G	B	G	B	G	B	G	
4	300	3·1	··	2·8	··	2·3	··	3·0	··	2·7	··	2·2	··	2·8	··	2·6	··	2·1	··	2·7	··	2·5	··	2·0	··	2·6	··	2·4	··	1·9	··	2·5	··	2·3	··	1·9	··	4
3	290	3·1	··	2·7	··	2·3	··	2·9	··	2·6	··	2·2	··	2·8	··	2·5	··	2·1	··	2·6	··	2·4	··	2·0	··	2·5	··	2·3	··	1·9	··	2·4	··	2·2	··	1·8	··	3
2	280	2·9	··	2·6	··	2·2	··	2·8	··	2·5	··	2·1	··	2·7	··	2·4	··	2·0	··	2·5	··	2·3	··	1·9	··	2·4	··	2·2	··	1·8	··	2·3	··	2·1	··	1·7	··	2
1	270	2·8	··	2·5	··	2·1	··	2·7	··	2·4	··	2·0	··	2·6	··	2·2	··	1·9	··	2·4	··	2·1	··	1·8	··	2·3	··	2·1	··	1·7	··	2·2	··	2·0	··	1·6	··	1
1	260	2·7	92·3	2·5	102·4	2·0	112·5	2·6	96·4	2·3	107·0	1·9	117·5	2·5	100·5	2·2	111·5	1·8	122·5	2·3	104·6	2·1	116·1	1·7	127·5	2·2	108·7	2·0	120·6	1·6	132·5	2·1	112·8	1·9	125·2	1·6	137·5	1
2	250	2·6	··	2·3	··	1·9	··	2·5	··	2·2	··	1·8	··	2·4	··	2·1	··	1·7	··	2·2	··	2·0	··	1·6	··	2·1	··	1·9	··	1·6	··	2·0	··	1·8	··	1·5	··	2
3	240	2·5	··	2·2	··	1·9	··	2·4	··	2·1	··	1·8	··	2·3	··	2·0	··	1·7	··	2·1	··	1·9	··	1·6	··	2·0	··	1·8	··	1·5	··	1·9	··	1·7	··	1·4	··	3
4	230	2·4	··	2·1	··	1·8	··	2·3	··	2·0	··	1·7	··	2·2	··	1·9	··	1·6	··	2·0	··	1·8	··	1·5	··	1·9	··	1·7	··	1·4	··	1·8	··	1·6	··	1·4	··	4
5	220	2·3	··	2·0	··	1·7	··	2·2	··	1·9	··	1·6	··	2·1	··	1·8	··	1·5	··	2·0	··	1·7	··	1·4	··	1·8	··	1·6	··	1·3	··	1·7	··	1·5	··	1·3	··	5
6	210	2·2	··	1·9	··	1·6	··	2·1	··	1·8	··	1·5	··	2·0	··	1·7	··	1·4	··	1·9	··	1·6	··	1·3	··	1·7	··	1·5	··	1·3	··	1·6	··	1·4	··	1·2	··	6
1	200	2·1	··	1·9	··	1·5	··	2·0	··	1·8	··	1·4	··	1·9	··	1·7	··	1·4	··	1·8	··	1·6	··	1·3	··	1·6	··	1·4	··	1·2	··	1·5	··	1·4	··	1·2	··	1
2	190	2·0	··	1·8	··	1·4	··	1·9	··	1·7	··	1·4	··	1·8	··	1·6	··	1·3	··	1·7	··	1·5	··	1·2	··	1·5	··	1·4	··	1·1	··	1·4	··	1·3	··	1·1	··	2
3	180	1·8	··	1·7	··	1·4	··	1·7	··	1·6	··	1·3	··	1·6	··	1·5	··	1·2	··	1·6	··	1·4	··	1·2	··	1·4	··	1·3	··	1·1	··	1·3	··	1·2	··	1·0	··	3
4	170	1·7	··	1·6	··	1·3	··	1·6	··	1·5	··	1·2	··	1·5	··	1·4	··	1·1	··	1·5	··	1·3	··	1·1	··	1·3	··	1·2	··	1·0	··	1·3	··	1·2	··	1·0	··	4

Above the Rule. Qualities on the Rule. Below the Rule.

working, I charged my copper with the raw barrels, as indicated by the pointing No. of the 3d quality, which gives 58·7 raw barrels. I then brought the copper to boil, and tested a sample by the Saccharometer, and found it to indicate 67·4 degs., being 1·8 degs. above 65·6 degs.—the required gravity of the raw worts. I then increased the barrels in the copper to 50·0 barrels, and tested a sample as before, and found it to be 65·6 degs., thus agreeing with the indication of the 2d quality of malt, viz. pointing No. 3·7 gives raw barrels, 50·0 at 65·6 degs.

```
E. 1. In Copper, Raw    brls. 50·0 at 65·6 degs.
      1¼ Hours, Boiled    „   46·0  „ 72·8   „
      In Tun,   Cold      „   37·6  „ 80·0   „
```

This Brewing was collected E. 6. in No. 3. tun, set temperature 55°, yeast 68 lb. or 5 lb. per quarter, fermented 9 days, attenuated to 36 degs., highest degree of temperature 63°.

The above may be a guide for all practical purposes.

Experimental.

By the two first divisions of the weights, and the graduated measure, may be defined the required weight, avoirdupois, of any soluble Saccharine matter. To give *in one barrel* one degree of gravity by the Saccharometer, the bulk of the weight of the Saccharine is included in the barrel or 36 galls.

	lb.	oz.	Gravity.	Deg.
Average West India Sugar,	1	0	in 1 brl.	1
„ East „	0	15	„	„
„ Lump „	0	15¼	„	„
„ Candy „	0	15	„	„
„ Molasses „	1	2½	„	„
„ Honey „	1	2¼	„	„
„ Manna „	1	2½	„	„

Instance.

Take the first weight of the second division, marked 1, $\frac{1}{36}$. which indicates one pound; or vary the order, and take the fifth weight, marked 1, $\frac{1}{36}$. which indicates one pound, or 36 pounds; likewise reading or varying the graduated measure. Saccharine matter weighed and dissolved thus, will, by the Saccharometer, indicate the degrees of specific gravity. The other weights of the second division, will read ³/₄, ½, ¼, and the *first* division, oz. in connection, according to the variation.

COST.

GRAY'S ALE BREWER'S ASSISTANT—THE PRACTICAL PART, ... £4 6 0

Should any purchaser of the practical part of the Instrument afterwards wish the experimental, he may have the same added, on returning the Instrument, at the cost of £2, 13s. 6d. and paying carriage to and from Edinburgh.

GRAY'S ALE BREWER'S ASSISTANT—PRACTICAL AND EXPERIMENTAL, . . £6 15 0

The under-stated Articles, if ordered, made at the following prices:—

A Small Mill,	from £0 5 0	to	£0 15 0
Beam and Scales,	„ 0 5 0	„	1 0 0
Copper, with Iron Furnace,	„ 1 0 0	„	1 10 0
Mash Tun, with Sparging Machine,	„ 0 10 0	„	0 10 0
Under Back,	„ 0 2 0	„	0 2 0
Cooler,	„ 0 3 0	„	0 5 0
Fermenting Tun,	„ 0 2 0	„	0 2 0
Casks,	„ 0 8 0	„	0 8 0
	£2 15 0		£4 12 0

Directions as to the Size of the above Articles, for those who may be inclined to furnish them for themselves.

Mill.—Small Coffee-Mill.

Beam and Scales.—Beam, 16 inches.

Copper.—Bottom, Cross, 9 inches,—mouth, 12 inches—depth, 12 inches.

Mash Tun.—Cross, 13 inches—depth, 12 inches.

Under Back.—Cross, 9 inches—depth, 9 inches.

Cooler.—Cross, 24 inches—depth, 5 inches.

Fermenting Tun.—Cross, 12 inches—depth, 14 inches.

Casks.—2 galls. each.

I would recommend malt to be from two to three months old before being used, and in Brewing high-priced Ale, take a quality on the Rules below the *actual* quality of the malt, (which will indicate fewer *barrels*,) so that the richest of the wort may go to the Ale—the afterings may be wrought up in low-priced Ale or Table Beer.

Printed by Libri Plureos GmbH in Hamburg,
Germany